Old Trees Have Secrets

TALKING CUB
Published by Speaking Tiger Books LLP
125A, Ground Floor, Shahpur Jat
New Delhi 110049

First published in paperback in Talking Cub by Speaking Tiger Books in 2023

ISBN: 978-93-5447-425-5
eISBN: 978-93-5447-455-2

10 9 8 7 6 5 4 3 2 1

Printed at : G.K. Fine Art Press

Old Trees Have Secrets

Ruskin Bond

Illustrated by David Yambem

talking CUB

An Imprint of Speaking Tiger Books

Old trees have secrets

They've seen it all

Children run down to the woods to play,
And a leopard is lurking in search of its prey.

Shepherds in search of their wandering sheep,
Friends asleep on the grass beneath

Old trees have secrets
They've seen it all

Armies that march to cities that fall,
Many there are who are kings for a day,
As soldiers keep coming from lands far away.

Storms come and go,
and sometimes the thunder
Lights up the sky,
and tears it asunder.

But the old tree still stands,
its trunk thick and strong,
As it patiently waits for
summer's sweet song.

Yes, old trees have secrets
They've seen it all happen,

The wedding band passing,
the beggar misshapen.

They've seen people happy, they've seen people sad,
They've seen the world peaceful, and they've seen it go mad.

Old trees have secrets
They've seen it all happening,

The birds still singing,
the river still running,
The folly of hate
and the joy of loving.

RUSKIN BOND is the author of numerous novels, short-story collections and non-fiction books, many of them classics. Among them are *When I Was a Boy*, *Lone Fox Dancing*, *The Room on the Roof*, *A Flight of Pigeons*, and *A Book of Simple Living*. He received the Sahitya Akademi Award in 1993, the Padma Shri in 1999 and the Padma Bhushan in 2014.

DAVID YAMBEM is an animator, illustrator and a visual storyteller from Manipur. He is a plant enthusiast, loves tea, cycling, cooking and watching nature documentary series.